~A BINGO BOOK~

Washington Bingo Book

COMPLETE BINGO GAME IN A BOOK

Written By Rebecca Stark

ISBN 978-0-87386-540-1

Educational Books 'n' Bingo

Printed in the U.S.A.

DIRECTIONS

INCLUDED:

List of Terms

Templates for Additional Terms and Clues

2 Clues per Term

30 Unique Bingo Cards

Markers

1. **Either cut apart the book or make copies of ALL the sheets. You might want to make an extra copy of the clue sheets to use for introduction and review. Keep the sheets in an envelope for easy reuse.**

2. Cut apart the call cards with terms and clues.

3. Pass out one bingo card per student. There are enough for a class of 30.

4. Pass out markers. You may cut apart the markers included in this book or use any other small items of your choice.

5. Decide whether or not you will require the entire card to be filled. Requiring the entire card to be filled provides a better review. However, if you have a short time to fill, you may prefer to have them do the just the border or some other format. Tell the class before you begin what is required.

6. There are 50 terms. Read the list before you begin. If there are any terms that have not been covered in class, you may want to read to the students the term and clues before you begin.

7. There is a blank space in the middle of each card. You can instruct the students to use it as a free space or you can write in answers to cover terms not included. Of course, in this case you would create your own clues. (Templates provided.)

8. Shuffle the cards and place them in a pile. Two or three clues are provided for each term. If you plan to play the game with the same group more than once, you might want to choose a different clue for each game. If not, you may choose to use more than one clue.

9. Be sure to keep the cards you have used for the present game in a separate pile. When a student calls, "Bingo," he or she will have to verify that the correct answers are on his or her card AND that the markers were placed in response to the proper questions. Pull out the cards that are on the student's card keeping them in the order they were used in the game. Read each clue as it was given and ask the student to identify the correct answer from his or her card.

10. If the student has the correct answers on the card AND has shown that they were marked in response to the *correct questions,* then that student is the winner and the game is over. If the student does not have the correct answers on the card OR he or she marked the answers in response to *the wrong questions,* then the game continues until there is a proper winner.

11. If you want to play again, reshuffle the cards and begin again.

Have fun!

TERMS INCLUDED

Apples

Blue Mountains

Bluebunch Wheatgrass

Border

Cascade Mountains

Chief Joseph

Climate

Columbia Mountains

Columbia River

Columbian Mammoth

Columbian Plateau

County (-ies)

Crops

Darner Dragonfly

Evergreen State

Executive Branch

Fish (-ing)

Flag

Fur(s)

Glacier(s)

Gold Rush

Grand Coulee

Industries

Judicial Branch

Lake(s)

Legislative Branch

Lewis and Clark

Livestock

Mount Rainier

Mount St. Helens

Okanogan Highlands

Olympia

Olympic Marmot

Olympic Peninsula

Orca(s)

Pacific Chorus Frog

Pacific Northwest

Petrified Wood

Puget Sound

Seattle

Song

Tacoma

Tri-Cities

Tribes

Union

Walla Walla

Washington Territory

Western Hemlock

Willapa Hills

Willow Goldfinch

Additional Terms

Choose as many additional terms as you would like and write them in the squares. Repeat each as desired.
Cut out the squares and randomly distribute them to the class.
Instruct the students to place their square on the center space of their card.

Washington Bingo

Clues for
Additional Terms

Write two clues for each of your additional terms.

1. 2.	1. 2.
1. 2.	1. 2.
1. 2.	1. 2.

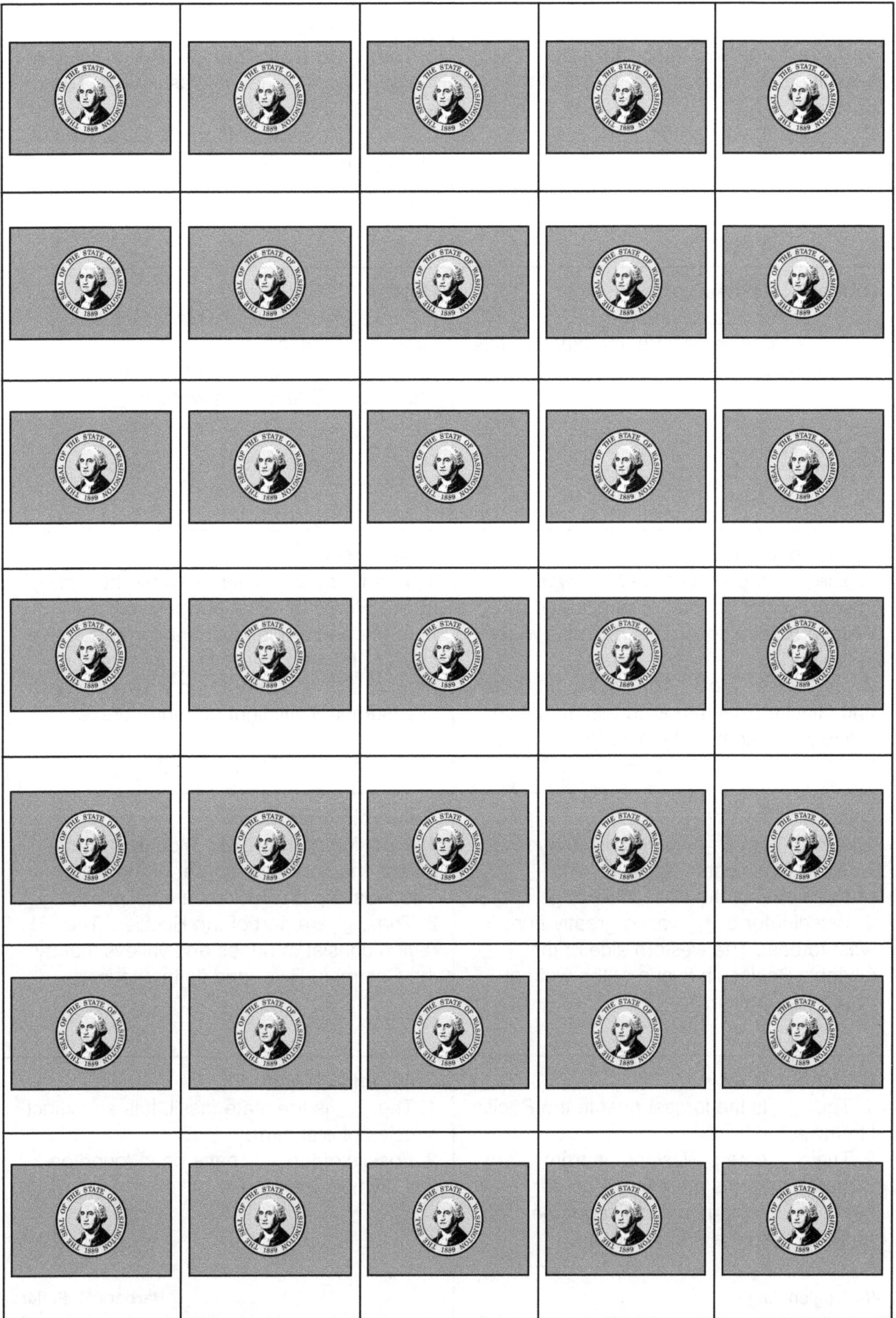

Apples
1. ___ are the most important crop. Washington produces about 64% of the nation's ___.
2. ___ are the state fruit.

Blue Mountains
1. The ___ are south of the Snake River in the southeast corner of Washington. They are mostly in Oregon.
2. The ___ are lower than the Cascades or the Olympic Mountains.

Bluebunch Wheatgrass
1. ___ is the state grass.
2. ___ is found in eastern Washington. It is well suited for grazing.

Border
1. Two states ___ Washington; they are Oregon and Idaho.
2. Canada is Washington's northern ___. The Pacific Ocean is its western ___

Cascade Mountains
1. The ___ are east of the Northwest Interior, Puget Sound Lowlands, and Willapa Hills regions. This region is wider in the north.
2. Mt. Rainier, Mount Adams, Mount Baker, and Glacier Peak are all in this mountain range in the center of the state.

Chief Joseph
1. This Nez Perce chief became the symbol of Nez Percé heroism and resistance.
2. At the end of his eloquent surrender speech, he said, "Hear me, my chiefs; my heart is sick and sad. From where the Sun now stands, I will fight no more forever."

Climate
1. A mild, humid ___ predominates in western Washington. A cooler, drier ___ prevails east of the Cascade Range.
2. Washington's ___ varies greatly from west to east. The western side of the Olympic Peninsula is one of the wettest area in the nation.

Columbia Mountains
1. A portion of the Rocky Mountains cuts across the northeast corner of the state. The Washington Rockies are called the ___.
2. The ___ are part of the Rockies. The region consist of ridges and valleys, cut by the Columbia River and its tributaries.

Columbia River
1. The ___ is the largest river in the Pacific Northwest.
2. The ___ enters Washington from Canada. It forms most of the border between Washington and Oregon before emptying into the Pacific Ocean.

Columbian Mammoth
1. The ___ is the state fossil. It is an extinct species of elephant.
2. Fossils of the ___ have been found on the Olympic Peninsula.

Columbian Plateau 1. Southeastern Washington is covered by the ___, also called the Columbian Basin. It is the area south and east of the great bend in the Columbia River. 2. Grand Coulee and Moses Coulee are notable canyons of the ___.	**County (-ies)** 1. There are 39 ___ in Washington. 2. King ___, which includes Seattle, is the largest.
Crops 1. About 70% of Washington's agricultural revenue comes from apples and other ___; the rest comes from livestock products. 2. The top ___ are apples, wheat, and potatoes.	**Darner Dragonfly** 1. The green ___ is the state insect. 2. The green ___ gets its name from its emerald green thorax. It is beneficial because it consumes a large number of insect pests.
Evergreen State 1. The official nickname of Washington is the ___. 2. Washington was given this nickname because of the because of the many large fir and pine trees.	**Executive Branch** 1. The ___ includes the governor, the lieutenant governor, the secretary of state, the treasurer, the attorney general, and four other elected officials. 2. The governor is head of the ___. The present-day governor is [fill in].
Fish (-ing) 1. ___ is a major industry in Washington state. A king salmon is depicted on the state quarter. 2. The steelhead trout is the state ___.	**Flag** 1. Washington has the only state ___ with a green field. 2. In the center of the ___'s green field is the Great Seal, which features a portrait of President Washington.* *Washington is the only state named in honor of a President.
Fur(s) 1. Eighteenth-century explorers in the Northwest traded with Native Americans for sea otter ___. 2. Hudson's Bay Company; the Northwest Company; the Pacific ___ Company; and the Rocky Mountain ___ Company were ___ traders. Washington Bingo	**Glacier(s)** 1. Washington has more ___ than any other state except Alaska. They are found on most of the state's high mountains. 2. North Cascades National Park has about 1,729 perennial snow or ice features with 85 named ___. © Barbara M. Peller

Gold Rush	Grand Coulee
1. Seattle was the staging area for the Klondike ___ of the 1890s. The Klondike ___ National Historical Park commemorates that role. 2. Seattle advertised itself as the place to outfit oneself for the ___. The resulting boom helped transform Seattle into the leading city of the Northwest.	1. The ___ Dam on the Columbia River was built to produce hydroelectric power and to provide irrigation. 2. The ___ provides 30% of the nation's hydroelectric power.
Industries	**Judicial Branch**
1. Fishing, lumber, and mining are important ___. 2. Transportation equipment, aircraft, and computer and electronic products are important manufactured products. Shipbuilding and food processing are also important ___.	1. The ___ is composed of the state courts, 2. The Supreme Court is the highest court of the ___.
Lake(s)	**Legislative Branch**
1. Chelan, Roosevelt, and Washington are some ___ in Washington. 2. ___ Chelan is the third deepest in the nation. The name is based on a Salish Indian word, *Tsi-Laan,* meaning "deep water."	1. The ___ of government comprises the Senate and the House of Representatives. 2. The ___ makes the laws.
Lewis and Clark	**Livestock**
1. The ___ Expedition is also known as the Corps of Discovery. It crossed into what is now the state of Washington in October 1805. 2. ___ had a difficult time navigating the Columbia River. They spent the winter at Fort Clatsop, on the Oregon side of the river.	1. Dairy products and beef cattle and calves are the top ___ products. 2. Dairy products, especially milk, are the most important ___ products.
Mount Rainier	**Mount St. Helens**
1. At 14,410 feet, ___ is the highest point in Washington. It is in the Cascade Mountains. 2. This glaciated peak is the fourth highest peak in the nation.	1. A major volcanic eruption of ___ occurred in 1980. 2. ___, the most active volcano in the United States, is in the Cascade Mountain range.

Okanogan Highlands 1. The ___ cover northerneastern Washington. This geographic region is bordered by Canada, the Columbian Plateau, the Cascade Mountains, and Idaho. 2. The Columbia, Okanogan, Sanpoi, Kettle, Pend Orielle, and Spokane are major rivers in the ___. Roosevelt Lake is in this region.	**Olympia** 1. The capital of Washington is ___. 2. This capital city is a major cultural center of the Puget Sound Region.
Olympic Marmot 1. The ___ is native to the Olympic Peninsula. Most of its habitat is protected within Olympic National Park. 2. This rodent has a long, bushy tail.	**Olympic Peninsula** 1. The ___ is south of the Strait of Juan de Fuca and west of Hood Canal. 2. The Olympic Mountains form the core of the ___. Cape Alava, the westernmost point in the contiguous* United States, and Cape Flattery, the northwesternmost point, are on the ___. *touching or connected throughout in an unbroken sequence
Orca(s) 1. The ___ is the state marine mammal. 2. Each year pods of orcas migrate through Puget Sound. Many tourists visit the state to watch them.	**Pacific Chorus Frog** 1. The ___ is the state amphibian. 2. This native amphibian can be found in every county of Washington.
Pacific Northwest 1. The ___ includes Oregon, Washington, and Idaho, as well as the Canadian province of British Columbia and territory of the Yukon. 2. Generally speaking, the ___ Region of North America is bounded by the Pacific Ocean to the west and the Rocky Mountains on the east.	**Petrified Wood** 1. ___ is called the state gem, but it is actually a fossil. 2. ___ can be seen in Ginkgo Petrified Forest State Park, Saddle Mountain, and Yakima Canyon.
Puget Sound 1. ___ is connected to the Pacific Ocean in the north by the Strait of Juan de Fuca. 2. The ___ Lowlands is a broad, low-lying region west of the Cascade Mountains. Tacoma and Olympia are in this region.	**Seattle** 1. ___ was the staging area for the Yukon Gold Rush. This helped make it the leading city of the Northwest. 2. ___ is the largest city in the Pacific Northwest. It is named for ___, chief of the Suquamish Indians.
Washington Bingo	© **Barbara M. Peller**

Song 1. "Washington, My Home" is the official state ___. 2. "Roll On Columbia, Roll On" is the official folk ___.	**Tacoma** 1. ___ is the third largest city in the state. It is located at the foot of Mount Rainier. 2. The city of ___ is on Commencement Bay. The Port of ___ occupies the south-eastern end and is the 7th largest container port in the nation.
Tri-Cities 1. ___ comprises the 3 cities located at the confluence of the Yakima, Snake, and Columbia rivers. 2. The ___ metropolitan area includes Kennewick, Pasco, and Richland. Nearby West Richland is usually included as well.	**Tribes** 1. At one time more than 100 distinct Native American ___ lived in the area. Today there are 29 federally recognized Indian ___ in the state. 2. The Yakama Indian Nation and the Colville Confederated ___ are the two largest Indian ___ in the state.
Union 1. Washington joined the ___ on November 11, 1889. 2. When Washington entered the ___, it became the 42nd state.	**Walla Walla** 1. The ___ sweet onion is the state vegetable. 2. ___ in southern Washington is famous for its sweet onions.
Washington Territory 1. ___ was carved out of the northern part of the Oregon Territory. 2. ___ existed from March 2, 1853, until November 11, 1889, when Washington was admitted to the Union as the 42nd state.	**Western Hemlock** 1. The ___ is the state tree. 2. This large coniferous tree is native to the West Coast.
Willapa Hills 1. The ___ are south of the Olympic Mountains and west of the Puget Sound Lowlands. 2. The Willapa Hills overlook Willapa Bay. The Olympic Mountains and ___ make up the Coastal Region.	**Willow Goldfinch** 1. The ___ is the state bird. 2. Also called the wild canary, the male of this species has a bright yellow body with black wings and tail and black on top of his head.

Washington Bingo

Washington Bingo

Petrified Wood	Apples	Bluebunch Wheatgrass	Flag	Cascade Mountains
Executive Branch	Blue Mountains	Western Hemlock	Mount St. Helens	Song
Washington Territory	Mount Rainier		Orca(s)	Willapa Hills
Walla Walla	Seattle	Union	Livestock	Olympia
Olympic Peninsula	Gold Rush	County (-ies)	Tribes	Lake(s)

Washington Bingo

Walla Walla	Washington Territory	Judicial Branch	Puget Sound	Lewis and Clark
Olympia	Darner Dragonfly	Industries	Seattle	Olympic Marmot
Columbia Mountains	Gold Rush		Columbian Mammoth	Union
Pacific Chorus Frog	Pacific Northwest	Mount Rainier	Willow Goldfinch	Cascade Mountains
Song	Western Hemlock	County (-ies)	Executive Branch	Tribes

Washington Bingo: Card No. 2

Washington Bingo

Gold Rush	Union	Darner Dragonfly	Livestock	Washington Territory
Olympia	Blue Mountains	Columbian Plateau	Apples	Glacier(s)
Seattle	Western Hemlock		Olympic Marmot	Border
Mount Rainier	Columbia Mountains	Olympic Peninsula	Pacific Chorus Frog	Judicial Branch
Tribes	Columbia River	County (-ies)	Willow Goldfinch	Lewis and Clark

Washington Bingo

Mount Rainier	Olympic Marmot	Bluebunch Wheatgrass	Columbia River	Lewis and Clark
Okanogan Highlands	Climate	Apples	Puget Sound	Washington Territory
Orca(s)	Pacific Chorus Frog		Lake(s)	Flag
Union	Blue Mountains	Western Hemlock	County (-ies)	Industries
Columbian Mammoth	Song	Chief Joseph	Tribes	Willapa Hills

Washington Bingo

Song	Cascade Mountains	Seattle	Industries	Columbia River
Okanogan Highlands	Union	Columbian Plateau	Columbian Mammoth	Blue Mountains
Bluebunch Wheatgrass	Willapa Hills		Mount St. Helens	Fur(s)
Lake(s)	Lewis and Clark	Petrified Wood	Willow Goldfinch	Crops
Darner Dragonfly	County (-ies)	Washington Territory	Mount Rainier	Orca(s)

Washington Bingo: Card No. 5

Washington Bingo

Border	Olympic Marmot	Judicial Branch	Lewis and Clark	Willapa Hills
Livestock	Seattle	Crops	Apples	Washington Territory
Puget Sound	Grand Coulee		Climate	Columbian Mammoth
County (-ies)	Olympic Peninsula	Willow Goldfinch	Chief Joseph	Bluebunch Wheatgrass
Olympia	Industries	Petrified Wood	Orca(s)	Evergreen State

Washington Bingo: Card No. 6

Washington Bingo

Petrified Wood	Olympic Marmot	Fur(s)	Union	Darner Dragonfly
Olympia	Lewis and Clark	Gold Rush	Blue Mountains	Okanogan Highlands
Willapa Hills	Flag		Columbian Mammoth	Climate
Mount Rainier	Pacific Chorus Frog	Columbian Plateau	Walla Walla	Columbia Mountains
County (-ies)	Columbia River	Willow Goldfinch	Chief Joseph	Border

Washington Bingo: Card No. 7

Washington Bingo

Orca(s)	Olympic Marmot	Fish (-ing)	Livestock	Climate
Okanogan Highlands	Bluebunch Wheatgrass	Puget Sound	Willapa Hills	Industries
Evergreen State	Columbia River		Lewis and Clark	Cascade Mountains
Tribes	Mount Rainier	Walla Walla	Columbian Mammoth	Pacific Chorus Frog
Western Hemlock	County (-ies)	Chief Joseph	Seattle	Olympia

Washington Bingo

Columbian Mammoth	Darner Dragonfly	Gold Rush	Evergreen State	Columbia River
Grand Coulee	Lewis and Clark	Orca(s)	Seattle	Olympic Marmot
Glacier(s)	Petrified Wood		Blue Mountains	Fish (-ing)
Crops	Cascade Mountains	Olympic Peninsula	Mount St. Helens	Fur(s)
Pacific Chorus Frog	Willow Goldfinch	Columbian Plateau	Walla Walla	Lake(s)

Washington Bingo

Walla Walla	Livestock	Climate	Puget Sound	Evergreen State
Willapa Hills	Industries	Apples	Blue Mountains	Lewis and Clark
Columbia River	Olympic Marmot		Flag	Columbia Mountains
Olympic Peninsula	Lake(s)	Crops	Willow Goldfinch	Glacier(s)
Columbian Plateau	Olympia	Judicial Branch	Song	Orca(s)

Washington Bingo

Border	Olympic Marmot	Seattle	Crops	Olympia
Fish (-ing)	Glacier(s)	Mount St. Helens	Columbian Mammoth	Apples
Okanogan Highlands	Lewis and Clark		Judicial Branch	Gold Rush
Columbian Plateau	Washington Territory	Willow Goldfinch	Columbia River	Walla Walla
Grand Coulee	County (-ies)	Petrified Wood	Chief Joseph	Darner Dragonfly

Washington Bingo

Darner Dragonfly	Cascade Mountains	Glacier(s)	Livestock	Columbian Mammoth
Gold Rush	Olympia	Bluebunch Wheatgrass	Chief Joseph	Blue Mountains
Petrified Wood	Fur(s)		Willapa Hills	Puget Sound
County (-ies)	Pacific Chorus Frog	Lewis and Clark	Walla Walla	Okanogan Highlands
Olympic Marmot	Fish (-ing)	Columbia River	Grand Coulee	Industries

Washington Bingo: Card No. 12

Washington Bingo

Crops	Cascade Mountains	Border	Glacier(s)	Willapa Hills
Bluebunch Wheatgrass	Fish (-ing)	Lewis and Clark	Columbian Mammoth	Columbia Mountains
Livestock	Industries		Gold Rush	Fur(s)
Orca(s)	Willow Goldfinch	Climate	Columbia River	Walla Walla
County (-ies)	Lake(s)	Chief Joseph	Petrified Wood	Mount St. Helens

Washington Bingo

Executive Branch	Lewis and Clark	Seattle	Grand Coulee	Columbian Mammoth
Industries	Petrified Wood	Glacier(s)	Blue Mountains	Olympic Marmot
Crops	Flag		Judicial Branch	Columbian Plateau
Lake(s)	Willow Goldfinch	Columbia River	Climate	Border
County (-ies)	Puget Sound	Columbia Mountains	Olympia	Orca(s)

Washington Bingo

Mount St. Helens	Columbian Mammoth	Seattle	Darner Dragonfly	Livestock
Border	Judicial Branch	Apples	Bluebunch Wheatgrass	Grand Coulee
Willapa Hills	Petrified Wood		Washington Territory	Olympic Marmot
County (-ies)	Glacier(s)	Fish (-ing)	Willow Goldfinch	Crops
Olympia	Pacific Chorus Frog	Chief Joseph	Evergreen State	Gold Rush

Washington Bingo: Card No. 15

Washington Bingo

Climate	Glacier(s)	Fish (-ing)	Evergreen State	Pacific Northwest
Puget Sound	Columbia Mountains	Fur(s)	Okanogan Highlands	Flag
Crops	Cascade Mountains		Willapa Hills	Gold Rush
Mount Rainier	Industries	County (-ies)	Mount St. Helens	Walla Walla
Grand Coulee	Tri-Cities	Chief Joseph	Pacific Chorus Frog	Olympic Marmot

Washington Bingo

Columbian Plateau	Tacoma	Legislative Branch	Glacier(s)	Executive Branch
Mount St. Helens	Grand Coulee	Willow Goldfinch	Flag	Fur(s)
Columbian Mammoth	Orca(s)		Tri-Cities	Fish (-ing)
Lake(s)	Olympia	Walla Walla	Seattle	Columbia Mountains
Olympic Peninsula	Crops	Darner Dragonfly	Livestock	Cascade Mountains

Washington Bingo

Evergreen State	Columbia River	Industries	Crops	Puget Sound
Olympic Marmot	Columbian Plateau	Olympic Peninsula	Willapa Hills	Grand Coulee
Columbian Mammoth	Columbia Mountains		Legislative Branch	Bluebunch Wheatgrass
Cascade Mountains	Apples	Willow Goldfinch	Walla Walla	Judicial Branch
Tri-Cities	Glacier(s)	Seattle	Tacoma	Border

Washington Bingo

Willapa Hills	Border	Glacier(s)	Fish (-ing)	Walla Walla
Mount St. Helens	Livestock	Olympic Marmot	Darner Dragonfly	Flag
Tacoma	Columbia River		Blue Mountains	Washington Territory
Judicial Branch	Tri-Cities	Olympic Peninsula	Pacific Chorus Frog	Legislative Branch
Bluebunch Wheatgrass	Pacific Northwest	Olympia	Orca(s)	Chief Joseph

Washington Bingo

Executive Branch	Tacoma	Livestock	Glacier(s)	Chief Joseph
Industries	Gold Rush	Okanogan Highlands	Olympic Peninsula	Puget Sound
Cascade Mountains	Fur(s)		Mount Rainier	Apples
Song	Western Hemlock	Tribes	Pacific Chorus Frog	Tri-Cities
Union	Orca(s)	Pacific Northwest	Walla Walla	Legislative Branch

Washington Bingo

Mount St. Helens	Border	Okanogan Highlands	Glacier(s)	Song
Cascade Mountains	Legislative Branch	Climate	Fish (-ing)	Petrified Wood
Columbia Mountains	Olympia		Tacoma	Seattle
Olympic Peninsula	Darner Dragonfly	Tri-Cities	Lake(s)	Orca(s)
Mount Rainier	Pacific Northwest	Chief Joseph	Columbian Plateau	Pacific Chorus Frog

Washington Bingo

Evergreen State	Judicial Branch	Legislative Branch	Bluebunch Wheatgrass	Crops
Puget Sound	Livestock	Washington Territory	Fish (-ing)	Blue Mountains
Industries	Flag		Petrified Wood	Fur(s)
Tri-Cities	Lake(s)	Pacific Chorus Frog	Apples	Okanogan Highlands
Pacific Northwest	Columbian Plateau	Tacoma	Columbia Mountains	Mount Rainier

Washington Bingo

Climate	Tacoma	Darner Dragonfly	Bluebunch Wheatgrass	Chief Joseph
Border	Executive Branch	Olympia	Mount St. Helens	Apples
Judicial Branch	Crops		Tribes	Petrified Wood
Columbia Mountains	Pacific Northwest	Tri-Cities	Columbian Plateau	Pacific Chorus Frog
Song	Western Hemlock	Orca(s)	Olympic Peninsula	Legislative Branch

Washington Bingo

Climate	Orca(s)	Executive Branch	Tacoma	Fish (-ing)
Legislative Branch	Chief Joseph	Okanogan Highlands	Puget Sound	Petrified Wood
Fur(s)	Evergreen State		Crops	Columbia Mountains
Song	Tribes	Tri-Cities	Columbian Plateau	Cascade Mountains
Union	Mount Rainier	Pacific Northwest	Livestock	Western Hemlock

Washington Bingo

Mount Rainier	Okanogan Highlands	Tacoma	Seattle	Legislative Branch
Apples	Cascade Mountains	Mount St. Helens	Climate	Blue Mountains
Lake(s)	Fish (-ing)		Tribes	Tri-Cities
Washington Territory	Song	Western Hemlock	Pacific Northwest	Flag
Chief Joseph	Executive Branch	Industries	Grand Coulee	Union

Washington Bingo

Legislative Branch	Tacoma	Judicial Branch	Puget Sound	Evergreen State
Olympic Peninsula	Livestock	Fish (-ing)	Executive Branch	Climate
Lake(s)	Tribes		Flag	Mount Rainier
Columbian Plateau	Bluebunch Wheatgrass	Song	Pacific Northwest	Tri-Cities
Fur(s)	Grand Coulee	Seattle	Western Hemlock	Union

Washington Bingo

Judicial Branch	Industries	Tacoma	Executive Branch	Gold Rush
Song	Tribes	Mount St. Helens	Tri-Cities	Blue Mountains
Willow Goldfinch	Western Hemlock		Pacific Northwest	Mount Rainier
Evergreen State	Border	Okanogan Highlands	Union	Apples
Grand Coulee	Flag	Legislative Branch	Washington Territory	Fur(s)

Washington Bingo

Judicial Branch	Executive Branch	Washington Territory	Tacoma	Climate
Gold Rush	Legislative Branch	Tribes	Puget Sound	Flag
Western Hemlock	Columbia Mountains		Fur(s)	Olympic Peninsula
Walla Walla	Evergreen State	Olympia	Pacific Northwest	Tri-Cities
Bluebunch Wheatgrass	Grand Coulee	Columbian Mammoth	Union	Song

Washington Bingo: Card No. 28

Washington Bingo

Legislative Branch	Executive Branch	Evergreen State	Mount St. Helens	Grand Coulee
Pacific Chorus Frog	Olympic Peninsula	Okanogan Highlands	Fur(s)	Washington Territory
Lake(s)	Tribes		Blue Mountains	Tacoma
Gold Rush	Song	Lewis and Clark	Pacific Northwest	Tri-Cities
Climate	Fish (-ing)	Union	Border	Western Hemlock

Washington Bingo

Columbia River	Tacoma	Puget Sound	Grand Coulee	Tri-Cities
Apples	Executive Branch	Judicial Branch	Flag	Blue Mountains
Lake(s)	Crops		Fur(s)	Okanogan Highlands
Union	Border	Bluebunch Wheatgrass	Pacific Northwest	Tribes
Song	Willapa Hills	Western Hemlock	Legislative Branch	Washington Territory

Washington Bingo: Card No. 30